Air Fryer Cookbook for Beginners

Easy and Delicious Low-Carb Recipes to Learn Cooking with Your Air Fryer on a Budget

Linda Wang

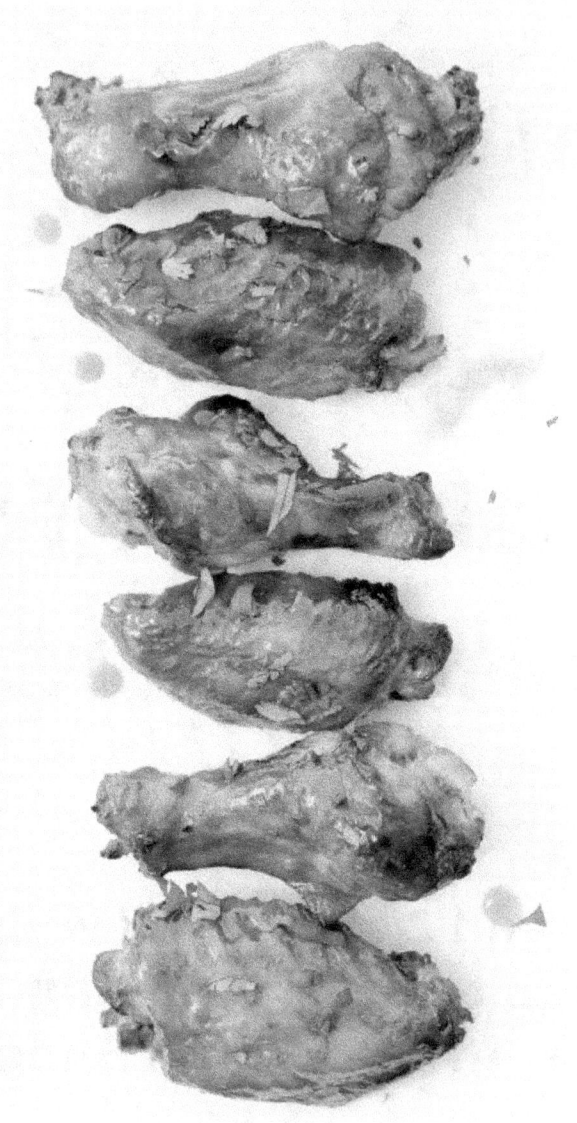

© **Copyright 2021 by Linda Wang - All rights reserved.**

The content contained within this book may not be reproduced, duplicated or transmitted without direct written permission from the author or the publisher.
Under no circumstances will any blame or legal responsibility be held against the publisher, or author, for any damages, reparation, or monetary loss due to the information contained within this book. Either directly or indirectly.

Legal Notice:
This book is copyright protected. This book is only for personal use. You cannot amend, distribute, sell, use, quote or paraphrase any part, or the content within this book, without the consent of the author or publisher.

Disclaimer Notice:
Please note the information contained within this document is for educational and entertainment purposes only. All effort has been executed to present accurate, up to date, and reliable, complete information. No warranties of any kind are declared or implied. Readers acknowledge that the author is not engaging in the rendering of legal, financial, medical or professional advice. The content within this book has been derived from various sources. Please consult a licensed professional before attempting any techniques outlined in this book.
By reading this document, the reader agrees that under no circumstances is the author responsible for any losses, direct or indirect, which are incurred as a result of the use of information contained within this document, including, but not limited to, — errors, omissions, or inaccuracies.

TABLE OF CONTENTS

INTRODUCTION 1

Asparagus Salad 5

Tomatoes and Swiss Chard Bake 7

Pork Stew 9

Chives Carrots and Onions 11

Ginger Mushrooms 12

Hot Buttery Dinner Rolls 14

Balsamic Cabbage 16

Kale and Walnuts 17

Turmeric Mushroom 19

Cilantro Roasted Cauliflower 21

Glazed Calamari 23

Pesto Almond Salmon 25

Tarragon and Parmesan Trout 27

Buttery Shrimp 29

Breaded Cod Sticks 31

Fish Nuggets 33

Salmon Fillets and Pineapple Mix 35

Herbed Tuna 36

Cilantro Trout Fillets 38

Lemon Pepper Chicken 39

Coconut Chicken Tenders	41
Lamb and Asparagus Mix	43
Flank Steak Beef	45
Crispy Lamb Recipe	47
Pork Loin with Potatoes	49
Simple Lamb Chops	51
Lamb Loin Chops with Lemon	53
Artichoke Spinach Casserole	55
Peanut Butter Cookies	57
Tofu with Capers Sauce	59
Tofu with Orange Sauce	62
Breadcrumbs Stuffed Mushrooms	64
Chinese Noodle Soup	66
Vegetable Noodle Soup	68
Kale Beef Soup	70
Chestnut Bacon Soup	72
Air fryer Mediterranean Chicken And Quinoa Stew	74
Lobster Bisque Soup	76
Faux Fried Pickles (Vegan)	78
Korean Grilled Chicken	80
Cheesy Meatballs	82
Cheesy Dinner Rolls	84
Cauliflower Rice and Plum Pudding	85

Apple Doughnuts 86

Tea Cookies 88

Zucchini Brownies 90

Raspberry Wontons 92

Coffee 'n Blueberry Cake 94

Melts in Your Mouth Caramel Cheesecake 97

Walnut Brownies 99

NOTES 101

INTRODUCTION

An Air Fryer is a magic revolutionized kitchen appliance that helps you fry with less or even no oil at all. This kind of product applies Rapid Air technology, which offers a new way to fry with less oil. This new invention cooks food through the circulation of superheated air and generates 80% low-fat food. Although the food is fried with less oil, you don't need to worry as the food processed by the Air Fryer still has the same taste like the food fried using the deep-frying method.

This technology uses a superheated element, which radiates heat close to the food and an exhaust fan in its lid to circulate airflow. An Air Fryer ensures that the food processed is cooked completely. The exhaust fan located at the top of the cooking chamber helps the food get the same heating temperature in every part quickly, resulting in a cooked food of better and healthier quality. Besides, cooking with an Air Fryer is also suitable for those individuals which are too busy or do not have enough time. For example, an Air Fryer only needs half a spoonful of oil and takes 10 minutes to serve a medium bowl of crispy French fries.

In addition to serving healthier food, an Air Fryer also provides some other benefits to you. Since an Air Fryer helps you fry using less oil or without oil for some kind of food, it automatically reduces the fat and cholesterol content in food. Indeed, no one will refuse to enjoy fried food without worrying about the greasy and fat content. Having fried food with no guilt is one of the pleasures of life. Besides having low fat and cholesterol, you save some amount of money by consuming oil sparingly, which can be used for other needs. An Air Fryer also can reheat your food. Sometimes, when you have fried leftover and you reheat it, it will usually serve reheated greasy food with some addition of unhealthy reuse oil. Undoubtedly, the saturated fat in the fried food gets worse because of this process. An Air Fryer helps you reheat your food without being afraid of extra oils that the food may absorb. Fried bananas, fish and chips, nuggets, or even fried chicken can be reheated to become as warm and crispy as they were before by using an Air Fryer.

Some people may think that spending some amount of money to buy a fryer is wasteful. I dare to say that they are wrong because an Air Fryer is not only used to fry. It is a sophisticated multi-function appliance since it also helps you to roast chicken, make steak, grill fish, and even bake a cake. With a built-in air filter, an Air Fryer filters the air and saves your kitchen from smoke and grease.

An air Fryer is really a new innovative method of cooking. Grab it fast and welcome to a clean and healthy kitchen.

Asparagus Salad

Preparation Time: 15 minutes

Servings: 4

Ingredients:

- 1 cup baby arugula
- 1 bunch asparagus; trimmed
- 1 tbsp. cheddar cheese; grated
- 1 tbsp. balsamic vinegar

- A pinch of salt and black pepper
- Cooking spray

Directions:

1. Put the asparagus in your air fryer's basket, grease with cooking spray, season with salt and pepper and cook at 360 °F for 10 minutes.
2. Take a bowl and mix the asparagus with the arugula and the vinegar, toss, divide between plates and serve hot with cheese sprinkled on top

Nutrition:

Calories: 200; Fat: 5g; Fiber: 1g; Carbs: 4g; Protein: 5g

Tomatoes and Swiss Chard Bake

Preparation Time: 20 minutes

Servings: 4

Ingredients:

- 3 oz. Swiss chard; chopped.
- 4 eggs; whisked
- 1 cup tomatoes; cubed
- 1 tsp. olive oil
- Salt and black pepper to taste.

Directions:

1. Take a bowl and mix the eggs with the rest of the ingredients except the oil and whisk well.
2. Grease a pan that fits the fryer with the oil, pour the swish chard mix and cook at 359 °F for 15 minutes.
3. Divide between plates and serve for breakfast

Nutrition:

Calories: 202; Fat: 14g; Fiber: 3g; Carbs: 5g; Protein: 12g

Pork Stew

Preparation Time: 35 minutes

Servings: 4

Ingredients:

- 1 eggplant; cubed
- 2 zucchinis; cubed
- 2 lb. pork stew meat; cubed
- ½ cup beef stock

- ½ tsp. smoked paprika
- Salt and black pepper to taste.
- A handful cilantro; chopped.

Directions:

1. In a pan that fits your air fryer, mix all the ingredients, toss, introduce in your air fryer and cook at 370 °F for 30 minutes
2. Divide into bowls and serve right away.

Nutrition:

Calories: 245; Fat: 12g; Fiber: 2g; Carbs: 5g; Protein: 14g

Chives Carrots and Onions

Preparation Time: 5 minutes

Cooking time: 20 minutes

Servings: 4

Ingredients:

- 2 red onions, sliced
- 1 pound baby carrots, peeled
- 1 tablespoon lime zest, grated
- 1 tablespoon balsamic vinegar
- 2 tablespoons chives, chopped

Directions:

1. In your air fryer's basket, combine the carrots with the onions and the other Ingredients, toss and cook at 320 degrees F for 20 minutes.
2. Divide between plates and serve as a side dish.

Nutrition:

Calories 132, fat 4, fiber 3, carbs 11, protein 4

Ginger Mushrooms

Preparation Time: 10 minutes

Cooking time: 20 minutes

Servings: 4

Ingredients:

- 2 tablespoons olive oil
- 2 tablespoons balsamic vinegar
- 2 pounds white mushrooms, halved
- 1 tablespoon ginger, grated
- 1 teaspoon cumin, ground
- A pinch of salt and black pepper

Directions:

1. In your air fryer's basket, combine the mushrooms with the oil, vinegar and the other ingredients, toss and cook at 360 degrees F for 20 minutes.
2. Divide the mix between plates and serve.

Nutrition:

Calories 182, fat 3, fiber 2, carbs 8, protein 4

Hot Buttery Dinner Rolls

Preparation Time: 3 hours 15 minutes

Servings: 6

Ingredients:

For the Rolls:

- 1 1/3 cups plain flour
- 1 ½ tablespoons white sugar
- 1 teaspoon of instant yeast
- 2 tablespoons melted butter
- 1/3 cup milk
- One Egg yolk
- A pinch of kosher salt
- A pinch of nutmeg

For the Topping:

- 2 tablespoons softened butter
- 2 tablespoons honey

Directions:

1. Mix the flour, sugar, instant yeast, and salt using a stand mixer. Whisk on low speed for 1 minute or until smooth.
2. Now; stir in the butter. Continue to mix for 1 more minute as it all combines.
3. Lay the dough onto a lightly floured surface and knead several times.
4. Transfer the dough to a large bowl, cover and place it in a warm room to rise until doubled in size.
5. Now; whisk the egg yolk with milk and nutmeg. Coat the balls with the egg mixture.
6. Shape into balls; loosely cover and allow the balls to rise until doubled, it takes about 1 hour.
7. Then; bake them in the preheated Air Fryer at 320 - degrees Fahrenheit for 14 to 15 minutes.
8. In the meantime; make the topping by simply mixing the very soft butter with honey. Afterward, spread the topping onto each warm roll.
9. Cover the leftovers and keep in your fridge.

Balsamic Cabbage

Preparation Time: 25 minutes

Servings: 4

Ingredients:

- 6 cups red cabbage; shredded
- 4 garlic cloves; minced
- 1 tbsp. balsamic vinegar
- 1 tbsp. olive oil
- Salt and black pepper to taste.

Directions:

1. In a pan that fits the air fryer, combine all the ingredients, toss, introduce the pan in the air fryer and cook at 380 °F for 15 minutes
2. Divide between plates and serve as a side dish.

Nutrition:

Calories: 151; Fat: 2g; Fiber: 3g; Carbs: 5g; Protein: 5g

Kale and Walnuts

Preparation Time: 20 minutes

Servings: 4

Ingredients:

- 3 garlic cloves
- 1/3 cup parmesan; grated
- 10 cups kale; roughly chopped.
- ½ cup almond milk
- ¼ cup walnuts; chopped.

- 1 tbsp. butter; melted
- ¼ tsp. nutmeg, ground
- Salt and black pepper to taste.

Directions:

1. In a pan that fits the air fryer, combine all the ingredients, toss, introduce the pan in the machine and cook at 360 °F for 15 minutes
2. Divide between plates and serve.

Nutrition:

Calories: 160; Fat: 7g; Fiber: 2g; Carbs: 4g; Protein: 5g

Turmeric Mushroom

Preparation Time: 20 minutes

Servings: 4

Ingredients:

- 1 lb. brown mushrooms
- ¼ tsp. cinnamon powder
- 4 garlic cloves; minced
- 1 tsp. olive oil

- ½ tsp. turmeric powder
- Salt and black pepper to taste.

Directions:

1. In a bowl, combine all the ingredients and toss.
2. Put the mushrooms in your air fryer's basket and cook at 370 °F for 15 minutes
3. Divide the mix between plates and serve as a side dish.

Nutrition:

Calories: 208; Fat: 7g; Fiber: 3g; Carbs: 5g; Protein: 7g

Cilantro Roasted Cauliflower

Preparation Time: 17 minutes

Servings: 4

Ingredients:

- 2 cups chopped cauliflower florets
- 2 tbsp. chopped cilantro
- 1 medium lime

- 2 tbsp. coconut oil; melted
- ½ tsp. garlic powder.
- 2 tsp. chili powder

Directions:

1. Take a large bowl, toss cauliflower with coconut oil. Sprinkle with chili powder and garlic powder. Place seasoned cauliflower into the air fryer basket
2. Adjust the temperature to 350 Degrees F and set the timer for 7 minutes
3. Cauliflower will be tender and begin to turn golden at the edges. Place into serving bowl. Cut the lime into quarters and squeeze juice over cauliflower. Garnish with cilantro.

Nutrition:

Calories: 73; Protein: 1.1g; Fiber: 1.1g; Fat: 6.5g; Carbs: 3.3g

Glazed Calamari

Preparation Time: 20 minutes

Cooking Time: 13 minutes

Servings: 3

Ingredients:

- ½ pound calamari tubes, cut into ¼ inch rings
- 1 cup flour
- 1 cup club soda
- ½ tablespoon red pepper flakes, crushed
- Salt and black pepper, to taste

For Sauce

- ½ cup honey
- 2 tablespoons Sriracha sauce
- ¼ teaspoon red pepper flakes, crushed

Directions:

1. Preheat the Air fryer to 375 degrees F and grease an Air fryer basket.
2. Soak the calamari in the club soda in a bowl and keep aside for about 10 minutes.

3. Mix flour, red pepper flakes, salt, and black pepper in another bowl.
4. Drain the club soda from calamari and coat the calamari rings evenly with flour mixture.
5. Arrange calamari rings into the Air fryer basket and cook for about 11 minutes.
6. Meanwhile, mix the honey, Sriracha sauce and red pepper flakes in a bowl.
7. Coat the calamari rings with the honey sauce and cook for 2 more minutes.
8. Dish out the calamari rings onto serving plates and serve hot.

Nutrition:

Calories: 307, Fats: 1.4g, Carbohydrates: 62.1g, Sugar: 35g, Proteins: 12g, Sodium: 131mg

Pesto Almond Salmon

Preparation Time: 17 minutes

Servings: 2

Ingredients:

- 2: 1 ½-inch-thick salmon fillets: about 4 oz. each
- ¼ cup sliced almonds, roughly chopped

- ¼ cup pesto
- 2 tbsp. unsalted butter; melted.

Directions:

1. In a small bowl, mix pesto and almonds. Set aside. Place fillets into a 6-inch round baking dish
2. Brush each fillet with butter and place half of the pesto mixture on the top of each fillet. Place dish into the air fryer basket. Adjust the temperature to 390 Degrees F and set the timer for 12 minutes
3. Salmon will easily flake when fully cooked and reach an internal temperature of at least 145 Degrees F. Serve warm.

Nutrition:

Calories: 433; Protein: 23.3g; Fiber: 2.4g; Fat: 34.0g; Carbs: 6.1g

Tarragon and Parmesan Trout

Preparation Time: 20 minutes

Servings: 4

Ingredients:

- 4 trout fillets; boneless
- ¾ cup parmesan; grated
- ½ cup chicken stock

- 2 garlic cloves; minced
- ¼ cup tarragon; chopped.
- 2 tbsp. olive oil
- Salt and black pepper to taste.

Directions:

1. In a pan that fits your air fryer, mix all the ingredients except the fish and the parmesan and whisk. Add the fish and grease it well with this mix
2. Sprinkle the parmesan on top, put the pan in the air fryer and cook at 380 °F for 15 minutes
3. Divide everything between plates and serve.

Nutrition:

Calories: 271; Fat: 12g; Fiber: 4g; Carbs: 6g; Protein: 11g

Buttery Shrimp

Preparation Time: 11 minutes

Servings: 2

Ingredients:

- 8 oz. medium shelled and deveined shrimp
- 2 tbsp. salted butter; melted.
- ¼ tsp. onion powder.
- ½ tsp. garlic powder.
- ½ tsp. Old Bay seasoning
- 1 tsp. paprika

Directions:

1. Toss all ingredients together in a large bowl. Place shrimp into the air fryer basket.
2. Adjust the temperature to 400 Degrees F and set the timer for 6 minutes. Turn the shrimp halfway through the cooking time to ensure even cooking. Serve immediately.

Nutrition:

Calories: 192; Protein: 16.6g; Fiber: 0.5g; Fat: 11.9g; Carbs: 2.5g

Breaded Cod Sticks

Preparation time: 15 minutes

Servings: 5

Ingredients:

- Large eggs: 2
- Milk: 3 tbsp.
- Breadcrumbs: 2 cups

- Black pepper: .5 tsp.
- Almond flour: 1 cup
- Salt: .25 tsp.
- Cod: 1 lb.

Directions:

1. Set the Air Fryer at 350º Fahrenheit.
2. Prepare three bowls; 1 with the milk and eggs; 1 with the pepper, salt, and breadcrumbs; and another with almond flour.
3. Dip the sticks in the flour, egg mixture, and lastly - the breadcrumbs.
4. Arrange in the basket and set the timer for 12 minutes – shaking halfway through the cooking process.
5. Serve with your favorite sauce.

Fish Nuggets

Preparation time: 30 minutes

Servings: 4

Ingredients:

- Eggs: 3
- Cod fillet: 1 lb.
- Olive oil: 4 tbsp.

- Almond flour: 1 cup
- Gluten-free breadcrumbs: 1 cup
- Salt: 1 tsp.

Directions:

1. Set the temperature of the Air Fryer at 390º Fahrenheit.
2. Cut the cod into nuggets.
3. Prepare three dishes. Beat the eggs in one. Combine the salt, oil, and breadcrumbs in another. The last one will be almond flour.
4. Cover each of the nuggets using the flour, a dip in the eggs, and the breadcrumbs.
5. Arrange the prepared nuggets in the basket and set the timer for 20 minutes. Serve.

Salmon Fillets and Pineapple Mix

Preparation Time: 15 minutes

Servings: 2

Ingredients:

- 2 medium salmon fillets; boneless
- 20 oz. canned pineapple pieces
- 2 tsp. garlic powder
- 1 tbsp. balsamic vinegar
- 1/2 tsp. ginger; grated
- A drizzle of olive oil
- Salt and black pepper to taste

Directions:

1. Grease a pan that fits your air fryer with the oil and add the fish inside.
2. Add the remaining ingredients and place the pan in the air fryer.
3. Cook at 350 °F for 10 minutes. Divide between plates and serve

Herbed Tuna

Preparation Time: 18 minutes

Servings: 4

Ingredients:

- 1 jalapeno pepper; chopped.
- 1/2 cup cilantro; chopped.
- 1/3 cup olive oil

- 2 tbsp. parsley; chopped.
- 1 tsp. red pepper flakes
- 2 tbsp. basil; chopped.
- 1 tsp. thyme; chopped.
- 4 sushi tuna steaks
- 3 garlic cloves; minced
- 1 small red onion; chopped.
- 3 tbsp. balsamic vinegar
- Salt and black pepper to taste

Directions:

1. Place all ingredients except the fish into a bowl and stir well.
2. Add the fish and toss, coating it well
3. Transfer everything to your air fryer and cook at 360 °F for 4 minutes on each side. Divide the fish between plates and serve

Cilantro Trout Fillets

Preparation Time: 18 minutes

Servings: 4

Ingredients:

- 4 trout fillets; boneless
- 1 cup black olives; pitted and chopped.
- 4 garlic cloves; minced
- 1 tbsp. olive oil
- 3 tbsp. cilantro; chopped.

Directions:

1. Add all of the ingredients to your air fryer and mix well
2. Cook at 360 °F for 6 minutes on each side. Divide everything between plates and serve.

Lemon Pepper Chicken

Cooking Time: 15 minutes

Servings: 1

Ingredients:

- 1 chicken breast
- 2 lemons; rind and juice part
- A handful of black peppercorns
- 1 tbsp. chicken seasoning
- 1 tsp. garlic purée
- Salt and pepper; to taste

Directions:

1. Preheat the air fryer to 356 °F. Place a large sheet of silver foil on a work top and place all the seasonings and the lemon rind inside
2. Lay out your chicken breasts onto a chopping board and trim off any fatty bits or bone. Season each side with salt and pepper

3. Rub the chicken seasoning into both sides. Afterwards, place chicken on the silver foil sheet and rub well.

4. Tightly seal the foil and flatten chicken further with a rolling pin. Then, place in the air fryer for 15 minutes until fully cooked in the middle. Serve.

Coconut Chicken Tenders

Cooking Time: 10 minutes

Servings: 5

Ingredients:

- 16 oz. chicken breast tenders
- 1 egg
- 1/4 cup light coconut milk
- 1/2 cup coconut flakes; sweetened
- 1/4 cup flour
- 1/2 cup panko breadcrumbs
- Oil spray
- 1/2 tsp. salt
- 1/2 tsp. ground ginger
- 1/2 tsp. onion powder
- 1/2 tsp. ground black pepper

Directions:

1. To prepare, rinse and pat the chicken tenders dry. Then, in 3 separate bowls, mix the following combinations: flour, salt, pepper, ground ginger

and onion powder; egg and light coconut milk; and panko crumbs and coconut flakes

2. One by one, dip the chicken tenders into the flour mixture first, then the egg mixture, then the panko mixture. Make sure the chicken is well-covered with each before moving on the next

3. Spray the bottom of your preheated basket with oil to prevent sticking. Lay chicken in a single layer into the basket and spray the tops lightly with oil. Air fry at 360 °F for 10 minutes, flipping once halfway through and spraying with oil once more. Serve once done

Lamb and Asparagus Mix

Preparation time: 10 minutes

Cooking time: 30 minutes

Servings: 4

Ingredients:

- 2 pounds lamb chops
- 2 tablespoons butter, melted
- 4 asparagus spears, trimmed and halved
- Salt and black pepper to the taste

- 1 tablespoon avocado oil
- ¼ cup beef stock
- 1 tablespoon dill, chopped

Directions:

1. In the air fryer's pan, mix the melted butter with the lamb chops and the other ingredients, toss and cook at 400 degrees F for 30 minutes.
2. Divide into bowls and serve.

Nutrition:

Calories 300, Fat 11, Fiber 4, Carbs 18, Protein 22

Flank Steak Beef

Preparation Time: 10 minutes

Cooking Time: 20 minutes

Servings: 4

Ingredients:

- 1 pound flank steaks, sliced
- 2 teaspoon vegetable oil
- ¼ cup xanthum gum
- ½ teaspoon ginger
- ½ cup soy sauce
- 1 tablespoon garlic, minced
- ½ cup water
- ¾ cup swerve, packed

Directions:

1. Preheat the Air fryer to 390 degrees F and grease an Air fryer basket.
2. Coat the steaks with xanthum gum on both the sides and transfer into the Air fryer basket.

3. Cook for about 10 minutes and dish out in a platter.
4. Meanwhile, cook rest of the ingredients for the sauce in a saucepan.
5. Bring to a boil and pour over the steak slices to serve.

Nutrition:

Calories: 372, Fat: 11.8g, Carbohydrates: 1.8g, Sugar: 27.3g, Protein: 34g, Sodium: 871mg

Crispy Lamb Recipe

Preparation Time: 40 Minutes

Servings: 4

Ingredients:

- 28-ounce rack of lamb
- 1 egg;
- 1 tbsp. bread crumbs
- 2 tbsp. macadamia nuts; toasted and crushed
- 1 tbsp. olive oil
- 1 tbsp. rosemary; chopped
- 1 garlic clove; minced
- Salt and black pepper to the taste

Directions:

1. In a bowl; mix oil with garlic and stir well
2. Season lamb with salt, pepper and brush with the oil.
3. In another bowl, mix nuts with breadcrumbs and rosemary

4. Put the egg in a separate bowl and whisk well.
5. Dip lamb in egg, then in macadamia mix, place them in your air fryer's basket, cook at 360 °F and cook for 25 minutes; increase heat to 400°F and cook for 5 minutes more. Divide among plates and serve right away

Pork Loin with Potatoes

Servings: 5

Preparation Time: 15 minutes

Cooking Time: 25 minutes

Ingredients

- 2 pounds pork loin
- 3 tablespoons olive oil, divided
- 1 teaspoon fresh parsley, chopped
- 3 large red potatoes, chopped
- ½ teaspoon garlic powder
- ½ teaspoon red pepper flakes, crushed
- Salt and ground black pepper, as required

Directions:

1. Coat the pork loin with oil and then, season evenly with parsley, salt, and black pepper.
2. In a large bowl, add the potatoes, remaining oil, garlic powder, red pepper flakes, salt, and black pepper and toss to coat well.

3. Set the temperature of air fryer to 325 degrees F. Grease an air fryer basket.
4. Place loin into the prepared air fryer basket.
5. Arrange potato pieces around the pork loin.
6. Air fry for about 25 minutes.
7. Remove from air fryer and transfer the pork loin onto a platter, wait for about 5 minutes before slicing.
8. Cut the pork loin into desired size slices and serve alongside the potatoes.

Nutrition:

Calories: 556, Carbohydrate: 29.6g, Protein: 44.9g, Fat: 28.3g, Sugar: 1.9g, Sodium: 132mg

Simple Lamb Chops

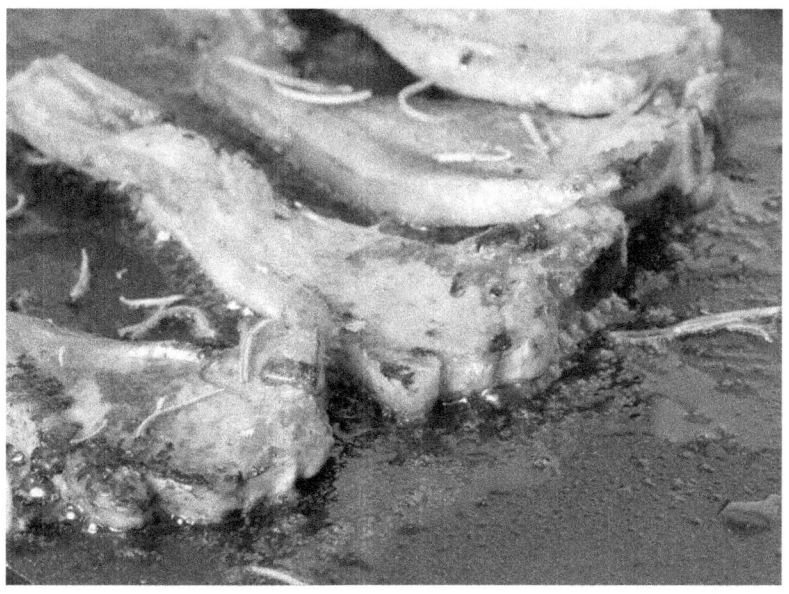

Servings: 2

Preparation Time: 10 minutes

Cooking Time: 6 minutes

Ingredients

- 1 tablespoon olive oil
- 4: 4-ounceslamb chops
- Salt and ground black pepper, as required

Directions:

1. In a large bowl, mix together the oil, salt, and black pepper.
2. Add the chops and coat evenly with the mixture.
3. Set the temperature of air fryer to 390 degrees F. Grease an air fryer basket.
4. Arrange chops into the prepared air fryer basket in a single layer.
5. Air fry for about 5-6 minutes.
6. Remove from air fryer and transfer the chops onto plates.
7. Serve hot.

Nutrition:

Calories: 486, Carbohydrate: 0.8g, Protein: 63.8g, Fat: 31.7g, Sugar: 0g, Sodium: 250mg

Lamb Loin Chops with Lemon

Servings: 4

Preparation Time: 15 minutes

Cooking Time: 30 minutes

Ingredients

- 2 tablespoons Dijon mustard
- 1 tablespoon fresh lemon juice
- 1 teaspoon dried tarragon
- ½ teaspoon olive oil
- 8: 4-ounceslamb loin chops
- Salt and ground black pepper, as required

Directions:

1. In a large bowl, mix together the mustard, lemon juice, oil, tarragon, salt, and black pepper.
2. Add chops and generously coat with the mixture.
3. Set the temperature of air fryer to 390 degrees F. Grease an air fryer basket.

4. Arrange chops into the prepared air fryer basket in a single layer in 2 batches.
5. Air fry for about 15 minutes, flipping once halfway through.
6. Remove the chops from air fryer and transfer onto serving plates.
7. Serve hot.

Nutrition:

Calories: 433, Carbohydrate: 0.6g, Protein: 64.1g, Fat: 17.6g, Sugar: 0.2g, Sodium: 201mg

Artichoke Spinach Casserole

Preparation Time: 30 minutes

Servings: 4

Ingredients:

- ⅓ cup full-fat mayonnaise
- 8 oz. full-fat cream cheese; softened.
- ⅓ cup full-fat sour cream.
- ¼ cup diced yellow onion
- ¼ cup chopped pickled jalapeños.
- 2 cups cauliflower florets; chopped
- 2 cups fresh spinach; chopped
- 1 cup artichoke hearts; chopped
- 1 tbsp. salted butter; melted.

Directions:

1. Take a large bowl, mix butter, onion, cream cheese, mayonnaise and sour cream. Fold in jalapeños, spinach, cauliflower and artichokes.

2. Pour the mixture into a 4-cup round baking dish. Cover with foil and place into the air fryer basket

3. Adjust the temperature to 370 Degrees F and set the timer for 15 minutes. In the last 2 minutes of cooking, remove the foil to brown the top. Serve warm.

Nutrition:

Calories: 423; Protein: 6.7g; Fiber: 5.3g; Fat: 36.3g; Carbs: 12.1g

Peanut Butter Cookies

Preparation Time: 13 minutes

Servings: 8

Ingredients:

- 1 large egg.
- ⅓ cup granular erythritol.
- 1 cup no-sugar-added smooth peanut butter.
- 1 tsp. vanilla extract.

Directions:

1. Take a large bowl, mix all ingredients until smooth. Continue stirring for 2 additional minutes and the mixture will begin to thicken.
2. Roll the mixture into eight balls and press gently down to flatten into 2-inch round disks.
3. Cut a piece of parchment to fit your air fryer and place it into the basket. Place the cookies onto the parchment, working in batches as necessary.
4. Adjust the temperature to 320 Degrees F and set the timer for 8 minutes.
5. Flip the cookies at the 6-minute mark. Serve completely cooled.

Nutrition:

Calories: 210; Protein: 8.8g; Fiber: 2.0g; Fat: 17.5g; Carbs: 14.1g

Tofu with Capers Sauce

Preparation Time: 10 minutes

Cooking Time: 27 minutes

Servings: 4

Ingredients:
- 4 tablespoons fresh parsley, divided
- 1 cup panko breadcrumbs
- 1: 14-ouncesblock extra-firm tofu, pressed and cut into 8 rectangular cutlets

- 2 teaspoons cornstarch
- 2 tablespoons capers
- ½ cup lemon juice
- 1 cup vegetable broth
- 2 garlic cloves, peeled
- ½ cup mayonnaise
- Salt and black pepper, to taste

Directions:

1. Preheat the Air fryer to 375 degrees F and grease an Air fryer basket.
2. Put half of lemon juice, 2 tablespoons parsley, 2 garlic cloves, salt and black pepper in a food processor and pulse until smooth.
3. Transfer the mixture into a bowl and marinate tofu in it.
4. Place the mayonnaise in a shallow bowl and put the panko breadcrumbs in another bowl.
5. Coat the tofu pieces with mayonnaise and then roll into the breadcrumbs.
6. Arrange the tofu pieces in the Air fryer pan and cook for about 20 minutes.

7. Mix broth, remaining lemon juice, remaining garlic, remaining parsley, cornstarch, salt and black pepper in a food processor and pulse until smooth.
8. Transfer the sauce into a small pan and stir in the capers.
9. Boil the sauce over medium heat and allow to simmer for about 7 minutes.
10. Dish out the tofu onto serving plates and drizzle with the caper sauce to serve.

Nutrition:

Calories: 307, Fat: 15.6g, Carbohydrates: 15.6g, Sugar: 3.4g, Protein: 10.8g, Sodium: 586mg

Tofu with Orange Sauce

Preparation Time: 20 minutes

Cooking Time: 20 minutes

Servings: 4

Ingredients:

- 1 pound extra-firm tofu, pressed and cubed
- 4 teaspoons cornstarch, divided
- ½ cup water
- 2 scallions: green part), chopped
- 1/3 cup fresh orange juice
- 1 tablespoon tamari
- 1 tablespoon honey
- 1 teaspoon orange zest, grated
- 1 teaspoon garlic, minced
- 1 teaspoon fresh ginger, minced
- ¼ teaspoon red pepper flakes, crushed

Directions:

1. Preheat the Air fryer to 390 degrees F and grease an Air fryer basket.
2. Mix the tofu, cornstarch, and tamari in a bowl and toss to coat well.
3. Arrange half of the tofu pieces in the Air fryer pan and cook for about 10 minutes.
4. Repeat with the remaining tofu and dish out in a bowl.
5. Put all the ingredients except scallions in a small pan over medium-high heat and bring to a boil.
6. Pour this sauce over the tofu and garnish with scallions to serve.

Nutrition:

Calories: 148, Fat: 6.7g, Carbohydrates: 13g, Sugar: 6.9g, Protein: 12.1g, Sodium: 263mg

Breadcrumbs Stuffed Mushrooms

Preparation Time: 25 minutes

Servings: 4

Ingredients:

- 16 small button mushrooms, stemmed and gills removed
- 1 ½ spelt bread slices
- 1 garlic clove; crushed
- 1 tbsp. flat-leaf parsley, finely chopped
- 1 ½ tbsp. olive oil
- Salt and ground black pepper; as your liking

Directions:

1. In a food processor, add the bread slices and pulse until fine crumbs form. Transfer the crumbs into a bowl. Add the garlic, parsley, salt and black pepper and stir to combine.
2. Stir in the olive oil. Set the temperature of air fryer to 390 °F. Grease an air fryer basket.

3. Stuff each mushroom cap with the breadcrumbs mixture.
4. Arrange mushroom caps into the prepared air fryer basket. Air fry for about 9 to 10 minutes.
5. Remove from air fryer and transfer the mushrooms onto a serving platter.
6. Set aside to cool slightly. Serve warm.

Chinese Noodle Soup

Preparation Time: 10 minutes

Cooking Time: 30 minutes

Servings: 8

Ingredients:

- 12 oz. noodles, cooked and drained
- 1 cup red bell peppers
- 1 cup broccoli
- 1 cup mushrooms
- 1 cup bok choy
- 4 green onion whites
- 8 garlic cloves, minced
- 1 inch ginger, minced
- 2 teaspoons soy sauce
- 1 teaspoon white chilli vinegar
- 20 oz. baby carrots
- 8 cups vegetable stock
- 2 teaspoons chilli sauce
- 2 tablespoons oil

- Salt and pepper, to taste
- Onion greens, for garnish

Directions:

1. Put the oil, ginger, garlic, baby carrots and onions in the Air fryer and select "Sauté".
2. Sauté for 4 minutes and add broccoli, bok choy, red bell peppers, mushrooms, soy sauce, chilli vinegar, chilli sauce and vegetable stock.
3. Set the Air fryer to "Soup" and cook for 15 minutes at high pressure.
4. Release the pressure naturally and add cooked noodles.
5. Season with salt and black pepper and garnish with onion greens.

Nutrition:

Calories: 145; Total Fat: 4.7g; Carbs: 22.6g; Sugars: 6.1g;Protein: 4g

Vegetable Noodle Soup

Preparation Time: 8 minutes

Cooking Time: 20 minutes

Servings: 5

Ingredients:

- ½ cup potatoes, diced
- ½ cup peas
- ½ cup cauliflower
- ½ cup carrots
- 6 oz. noodles, cooked and drained
- ½ cup onions
- 3 garlic cloves, minced
- ½ inch ginger, minced
- 1 cup tomatoes, diced
- 10 oz. baby carrots
- 2 teaspoons Worcestershire sauce
- 32 oz. vegetable stock
- 1 tablespoon olive oil
- 1 teaspoon salt
- 1 teaspoon black pepper

Directions:

1. Put the oil, ginger, garlic, carrots, onions and cauliflowers in the Air fryer and select "Sauté".
2. Sauté for 5 minutes and add potatoes, tomatoes, peas, vegetable stock and Worcestershire sauce.
3. Set the Air fryer to "Soup" and cook for 12 minutes at high pressure.
4. Release the pressure naturally and add cooked noodles.
5. Season with salt and black pepper and serve immediately.

Nutrition:

Calories: 148; Total Fat: 4g; Carbs: 24.8g; Sugars: 7.8g; Protein: 4.6g

Kale Beef Soup

Preparation Time: 15 minutes

Cooking Time: 43 minutes

Servings: 4

Ingredients:

- 1 lb. beef stew meat
- 3 garlic cloves, crushed
- 1 tsp. cayenne pepper
- 4 cups chicken broth
- 2 tbsp. olive oil
- 1 cup kale, chopped
- 1 onion, sliced
- ¼ tsp. black pepper
- ½ tsp. salt

Directions:

1. Add oil into air fryer and set on Sauté mode.
2. Add garlic and onion. Sauté for 3 minutes.
3. Add meat and sauté for 5 minutes.

4. Add broth and season with cayenne pepper, pepper and salt. Stir well.
5. Secure pot with lid and cook on manual high pressure for 25 minutes.
6. Quick release pressure then open the lid.
7. Add kale and stir well. Sit for 10 minutes.
8. Stir well and serve.

Nutrition:

Calories – 333 Protein – 40.3 g. Fat – 15.6 g. Carbs – 6.3 g.

Chestnut Bacon Soup

Preparation Time: 10 minutes

Cooking Time: 35 minutes

Servings: 4

Ingredients:

- 5 meatless bacon strips, cooked crispy
- 1 bay laurel leaf
- 3 tablespoons butter
- ½ pound fresh chestnuts
- 1 onion, chopped
- 1 potato, chopped
- 1 sprig sage
- ¼ teaspoon white pepper
- ¼ teaspoon nutmeg
- 2 tablespoons fresh cream

Directions:

1. Puree the fresh chestnuts in a blender.

2. Put the butter, onions, sage, celery and white pepper in the Air fryer and select "Sauté".
3. Sauté for 4 minutes and add potato, bay laurel leaf, stock and chestnuts.
4. Set the Air fryer to "Soup" and cook for 20 minutes at high pressure.
5. Release the pressure naturally and add nutmeg and fresh cream.
6. Blend the contents of the Air fryer to a smooth consistency and serve with bacon.

Nutrition:

Calories: 435; Total Fat: 25.4g; Carbs: 37.7g; Sugars: 2.4g;Protein: 16.7g

Air fryer Mediterranean Chicken And Quinoa Stew

Preparation Time: 10 minutes

Cooking Time: 20 minutes

Servings: 6

Ingredients:

- 1-¼ pounds of chicken thighs, boneless and skinless
- 1 cup yellow onion, chopped
- 4 cups of butternut squash, peeled and chopped
- 4 cups unsalted chicken stock
- 2 garlic cloves, chopped
- 1 bay leaf
- 1-¼ teaspoons of kosher salt
- 1 teaspoon of dried oregano
- 1 teaspoon of ground fennel seeds
- ½ cup of uncooked quinoa
- 1-ounce of olives, sliced and pitted

Directions:

1. Combine the chicken, squash, stock, onion, garlic, bay leaf, salt, ground fennel seeds, oregano, and pepper in your air fryer. Cover the lid, turn the valve to seal and cook on high pressure for 8 minutes.
2. Release the valve carefully, using mitts or tongs. Quick-release until the steam and pressure go down. Remove chicken, then add quinoa to the air fryer, turn to saute and cook while occasionally stirring until the quinoa is tender.
3. Shred the chicken and stir into stew. Discard bay leaf.
4. Serve the soup up into separate bowls, and sprinkle sliced olives.

Nutrition:

Calories – 243 Protein – 25 g. Fat – 6 g. Carbs – 24 g.

Lobster Bisque Soup

Preparation Time: 5 minutes

Cooking Time: 15 minutes

Servings: 4

Ingredients:
- 1 cups frozen or fresh lobster meat
- 1/2 cup homemade low-sodium vegetable or fish broth
- 1/4 cups unsweetened coconut cream
- 1 medium yellow or red onion, finely chopped
- 1 Tablespoons organic ghee (clarified butter)
- 2 garlic cloves, minced
- 1/2 cup dry white wine
- 1/2 cup carrots, finely chopped
- 1/2 cup celery, finely chopped
- 1/2 Tablespoon Worcestershire sauce
- 1/2 teaspoon smoked paprika or regular paprika
- 1/2 Tablespoon fresh parsley, chopped
- 1/2 teaspoon dried thyme
- Pinch of salt, pepper

Directions

1. Choose "Sauté" function on Air fryer. Add the ghee.
2. Once melted, add onion, celery, carrots, garlic. Cook 5 minutes.
3. Deglaze Air fryer with the wine. Simmer until reduced by half.
4. Stir in lobster meat, and broth.
5. Close, seal the lid. Press "Steam" function. Cook on HIGH 5 minutes.
6. When done, naturally release pressure. Remove the lid.
7. Stir in coconut cream, Worcestershire sauce, paprika, parsley, thyme, salt, and black pepper. Use an immersion blender to puree soup until smooth.
8. Ladle soup in bowls. Garnish with parsley, fresh ground black pepper. Serve.

Nutrition

Calories: 394, Fat: 29.3g , Carbohydrates: 5.3g, Fiber: 0.67g, Protein: 24.4g

Faux Fried Pickles (Vegan)

Servings: 1

Cooking Time: 5 minutes

Ingredients:

- 1 egg, beaten
- 1 cup pickle slices
- ½ cup grated Parmesan cheese

- ½ cup almond flour
- ¼ cup pork rinds, crushed
- Salt and pepper, to taste

Directions

1. Place the pickles in a bowl and pour the beaten egg over the top. Allow to soak.
2. In another dish or bowl, combine the Parmesan cheese, almond flour, pork rinds, salt, and pepper.
3. Dredge the pickles in the Parmesan cheese mixture and place on the double layer rack.
4. Place the rack with the pickles inside of the air fryer.
5. Close the lid and cook for 5 minutes at 390 degrees F.

Nutrition

Calories: 664; Carbs: 17.9g; Protein: 42g; Fat: 49.9g

Korean Grilled Chicken

Servings: 4

Cooking Time: 30 minutes

Ingredients:

- 2 pounds chicken wings
- ½ teaspoon fresh ground black pepper
- 1 teaspoon salt

- ½ cup gochujang
- 1 scallion, sliced thinly

Directions

1. Place in a Ziploc bag the chicken wings, salt, pepper, and gochujang sauce.
2. Allow marinating in the fridge for at least 2 hours.
3. Preheat the air fryer at 375 degrees F.
4. Place the grill pan accessory in the air fryer.
5. Grill the chicken wings for 30 minutes, making sure to flip the chicken every 10 minutes.
6. Top with scallions and serve with more gochujang.

Nutrition

Calories: 289; Carbs: 0.8g; Protein: 50.1g; Fat: 8.2g

Cheesy Meatballs

Preparation Time: 30 minutes

Servings: 16 meatballs

Ingredients:

- 1 large egg.
- 1 lb. 80/20 ground beef.
- 3 oz. low-moisture, whole-milk mozzarella, cubed
- ½ cup low-carb, no-sugar-added pasta sauce.
- ¼ cup grated Parmesan cheese.
- ¼ cup blanched finely ground almond flour.
- ¼ tsp. onion powder.
- 1 tsp. dried parsley.
- ½ tsp. garlic powder.

Directions:

1. Take a large bowl, add ground beef, almond flour, parsley, garlic powder, onion powder and egg. Fold ingredients together until fully combined

2. Form the mixture into 2-inch balls and use your thumb or a spoon to create an indent in the center of each meatball. Place a cube of cheese in the center and form the ball around it.
3. Place the meatballs into the air fryer, working in batches if necessary. Adjust the temperature to 350 Degrees F and set the timer for 15 minutes
4. Meatballs will be slightly crispy on the outside and fully cooked when at least 180 Degrees F internally.
5. When they are finished cooking, toss the meatballs in the sauce and sprinkle with grated Parmesan for serving.

Nutrition:

Calories: 447; Protein: 29.6g; Fiber: 1.8g; Fat: 29.7g; Carbs: 5.4g

Cheesy Dinner Rolls

Preparation Time: 10 minutes

Cooking Time: 5 minutes

Servings: 2

Ingredients:

- 2 dinner rolls
- ½ cup Parmesan cheese, grated
- 2 tablespoons unsalted butter, melted
- ½ teaspoon garlic bread seasoning mix

Directions:

1. Preheat the Air fryer to 355 degrees F and grease an Air fryer basket.
2. Cut the dinner rolls in slits and stuff cheese in the slits.
3. Top with butter and garlic bread seasoning mix.
4. Arrange the dinner rolls into the Air fryer basket and cook for about 5 minutes.
5. Dish out in a platter and serve hot.

Nutrition:

Calories: 608, Fat: 33.1g, Carbohydrates: 48.8g, Sugar: 4.8g, Protein: 33.5g, Sodium: 2000mg

Cauliflower Rice and Plum Pudding

Preparation Time: 30 minutes

Servings: 4

Ingredients:

- 4 plums, pitted and roughly chopped.
- 1 ½ cups cauliflower rice
- 2 cups coconut milk
- 2 tbsp. ghee; melted
- 3 tbsp. stevia

Directions:

1. Take a bowl, mix all the ingredients, toss, divide into ramekins, put them in the air fryer, and cook at 340 °F for 25 minutes. Cool down and serve

Nutrition:

Calories: 221; Fat: 4g; Fiber: 1g; Carbs: 3g; Protein: 3g

Apple Doughnuts

Preparation Time: 20 minutes

Cooking Time: 5 minutes

Servings: 6

Ingredients:

- 2½ cups plus 2 tablespoons all-purpose flour
- 1 egg
- 1½ teaspoons baking powder
- 2 tablespoons unsalted butter, softened
- ½ pink lady apple, peeled, cored and grated
- 1 cup apple cider
- ½ teaspoon ground cinnamon
- ½ cup brown sugar
- ½ teaspoon salt

Directions:

1. Preheat the Air fryer to 360 degrees F and grease an Air fryer basket lightly.
2. Boil apple cider in a medium pan over medium-high heat and reduce the heat.

3. Let it simmer for about 15 minutes and dish out in a bowl.
4. Sift together flour, baking powder, baking soda, cinnamon, and salt in a large bowl.
5. Mix the brown sugar, egg, cooled apple cider and butter in another bowl.
6. Stir in the flour mixture and grated apple and mix to form a dough.
7. Wrap the dough with a plastic wrap and refrigerate for about 30 minutes.
8. Roll the dough into 1-inch thickness and cut the doughnuts with a doughnut cutter.
9. Arrange the doughnuts into the Air fryer basket and cook for about 5 minutes, flipping once in between.
10. Dish out and serve warm.

Nutrition:

Calories: 433, Fat: 11g, Carbohydrates: 78.3g, Sugar: 35g, Protein: 6.8g, Sodium: 383mg

Tea Cookies

Preparation Time: 15 minutes

Cooking Time: 25 minutes

Servings: 15

Ingredients:

- 1 organic egg
- ½ cup salted butter, softened
- 2 cups almond meal
- 1 teaspoon ground cinnamon
- 2 teaspoons sugar
- 1 teaspoon organic vanilla extract

Directions:

1. Preheat the Air fryer to 370 degrees F and grease an Air fryer basket.
2. Mix all the ingredients in a bowl until well combined.
3. Make equal-sized balls from the mixture and transfer in the Air fryer basket.

4. Cook for about 5 minutes and press down each ball with fork.
5. Cook for about 20 minutes and allow the cookies cool to serve with tea.

Nutrition:

Calories: 291, Fat: 14g, Carbohydrates: 30.3g, Sugar: 2.3g, Protein: 11.9g, Sodium: 266mg

Zucchini Brownies

Preparation Time: 5 minutes

Cooking Time: 35 minutes

Servings: 12

Ingredients:

- 1 cup butter
- 1 cup dark chocolate chips
- 1½ cups zucchini, shredded
- ¼ teaspoon baking soda
- 1 egg
- 1 teaspoon vanilla extract
- 1/3 cup applesauce, unsweetened
- 1 teaspoon ground cinnamon
- ½ teaspoon ground nutmeg

Directions:

1. Preheat the Air fryer to 345 °F and grease 3 large ramekins.

2. Mix all the ingredients in a large bowl until well combined.
3. Pour evenly into the prepared ramekins and smooth the top surface with the back of spatula.
4. Transfer the ramekin in the Air fryer basket and cook for about 35 minutes.
5. Dish out and cut into slices to serve.

Nutrition:

Calories: 195, Fat: 18.4g, Carbohydrates: 8.2g, Sugar: 6.4g, Protein: 1.5g, Sodium: 143mg

Raspberry Wontons

Preparation Time: 36 minutes

Servings: 12

Ingredients:

For Wonton Wrappers:

- 18-oz cream cheese; softened
- 1 package of wonton wrappers
- 1/2 cup powdered sugar
- 1 tsp. vanilla extract

For Raspberry Syrup:

- 1: 12-ozpackage frozen raspberries
- 1/4 cup water
- 1 tsp. vanilla extract
- 1/4 cup sugar

Directions:

1. For wrappers: in a bowl; add the sugar, cream cheese and vanilla extract and whisk until smooth. Place a wonton wrapper onto a smooth surface. Place one tbsp. of cream cheese

mixture in the center of each wrapper. With wet fingers, fold wrappers around the filling and then, pinch the edges to seal

2. Set the temperature of air fryer to 350 °F. Lightly, grease an air fryer basket. Arrange wonton wrappers into the prepared air fryer basket in 2 batches

3. Air fry for about 8 minutes. Meanwhile; for the syrup: in a medium skillet, add water, sugar, raspberries and vanilla extract over medium heat and cook for about 5 minutes, stirring continuously

4. Remove from the heat and set aside to cool slightly. Transfer the mixture into food processor and blend until smooth. Remove the wontons from air fryer and transfer onto a platter. Serve the wontons with topping of raspberry syrup.

Coffee 'n Blueberry Cake

Servings: 6

Cooking Time: 35 minutes

Ingredients

- 1 cup white sugar
- 1/2 cup butter, softened
- 1 egg

- 1/2 cup sour cream
- 1/2 cup fresh or frozen blueberries
- 1/2 teaspoon baking powder
- 1/2 teaspoon ground cinnamon
- 1/2 teaspoon vanilla extract
- 1/4 cup brown sugar
- 1/4 cup chopped pecans
- 1/8 teaspoon salt
- 1-1/2 teaspoons confectioners' sugar for dusting
- 3/4 cup and 1 tablespoon all-purpose flour

Directions:

1. In a small bowl, whisk well pecans, cinnamon, and brown sugar.
2. In a blender, blend well all wet Ingredients. Add dry Ingredients except for confectioner's sugar and blueberries. Blend well until smooth and creamy.
3. Lightly grease baking pan of air fryer with cooking spray.

4. Pour half of batter in pan. Sprinkle half of pecan mixture on top. Pour the remaining batter. And then topped with remaining pecan mixture.
5. Cover pan with foil.
6. For 35 minutes, cook on 330 °F.
7. Serve and enjoy with a dusting of confectioner's sugar.

Nutrition:

Calories: 471; Carbs: 59.5g; Protein: 4.1g; Fat: 24.0g

Melts in Your Mouth Caramel Cheesecake

Servings: 8

Cooking Time: 40 minutes

Ingredients

- 1 Can Dulce de Leche
- 1 Tbsp Melted Chocolate
- Large Eggs
- 1 Tbsp Vanilla Essence
- 250 g Caster Sugar
- 50 g Melted Butter
- 500 g Soft Cheese
- Digestives, crumbled

Directions:

1. Lightly grease baking pan of air fryer with cooking spray. Mix and press crumbled digestives and melted butter on pan bottom. Spread dulce de leche.

2. In bowl, beat well soft cheese and sugar until fluffy. Stir in vanilla and egg. Pour over dulce de leche.
3. Cover pan with foil. For 15 minutes, cook on 390 °F.
4. Cook for 10 minutes at 330 °F. And then 15 minutes at 300 °F.
5. Let it cool completely in air fryer. Refrigerate for at least 4 hours before slicing.
6. Serve and enjoy.

Nutrition:

Calories: 463; Carbs: 44.1g; Protein: 17.9g; Fat: 23.8g

Walnut Brownies

Servings: 4

Preparation Time: 15 minutes

Cooking Time: 22 minutes

Ingredients

- ½ cup chocolate, roughly chopped
- 1/3 cup butter
- 5 tablespoons sugar
- 1 egg, beaten
- 1 teaspoon vanilla extract
- 5 tablespoons self-rising flour
- ¼ cup walnuts, chopped
- A pinch of salt

Directions:

1. In a microwave-safe bowl, add the chocolate and butter. Microwave on high heat for about 2 minutes, stirring after every 30 seconds.
2. Remove from microwave and set aside to cool.

3. Now, in a bowl, add the sugar, egg, vanilla extract, and salt and whisk until creamy and light.
4. Add the chocolate mixture and whisk until well combined.
5. Add the flour, and walnuts and mix until well combined.
6. Set the temperature of air fryer to 355 degrees F. Line a baking pan with a greased parchment paper.
7. Place mixture evenly into the prepared pan and with the back of spatula, smooth the top surface.
8. Arrange the baking pan into an air fryer basket.
9. Air fry for about 20 minutes.
10. Remove the baking pan from air fryer and set aside to cool completely.
11. Cut into 4 equal-sized squares and serve.

Nutrition:

Calories: 205, Carbohydrate: 1g, Protein: 3.1g, Fat: 13.8g, Sugar: 13.1g, Sodium: 91mg

Notes

www.ingramcontent.com/pod-product-compliance
Lightning Source LLC
Chambersburg PA
CBHW070933080526
44589CB00013B/1493